GEO

8.17
Lexile: _____

AR/BL: _____

AR Points: _____

SCIENCE PROJECT IDEAS

Science Project Ideas in
THE HOUSE
Revised Edition

Robert Gardner

Enslow Publishers, Inc.

40 Industrial Road   PO Box 38
Box 398   Aldershot
Berkeley Heights, NJ 07922   Hants GU12 6BP
USA   UK

http://www.enslow.com

Library of Congress Cataloging-in-Publication Data

Gardner, Robert, 1929–
    Science project ideas in the house / Robert Gardner.— Rev. ed.
        p. cm. — (Science project ideas)
    Originally published as: Science around the house.
    Includes bibliographical references and index.
    ISBN 0-7660-1705-2
    1. Science—Experiments—Juvenile literature. 2. Physics—
Experiments—Juvenile literature. 3. Scientific recreations—Juvenile
literature. [1. Science—Experiments. 2. Experiments. 3. Science projects.]
I. Title.
    Q164 .G34 2002
    507'.8—dc21

                                                        2001000700

Printed in the United States of America

This book was originally published in 1985 by Julian Messner as *Science
Around the House*.

10 9 8 7 6 5 4 3 2 1

To Our Readers:
We have done our best to make sure all Internet addresses in this book were
active and appropriate when we went to press. However, the author and the
publisher have no control over and assume no liability for the material available
on those Internet sites or on other Web sites they may link to. Any comments or
suggestions can be sent by e-mail to comments@enslow.com or to the address on
the back cover.

Illustration Credits: Stephen F. Delisle, pp. 86, 111; Enslow
Publishers, Inc., pp. 35, 71, 72; Gary Koellhoffer, Crooked Grin Design,
pp. 13, 14, 15, 20, 21, 25, 29, 67, 76, 80, 90, 103, 115, 117, 120; Stephanie
Rowland, pp. 7, 10, 17, 18, 98.

Cover Photo: © Corel Corporation (background), Jerry McCrea
(foreground).

CONTENTS

INTRODUCTION

Your home, in addition to being a place to eat, sleep, and live, is a good environment in which to carry out science experiments. Your kitchen has hot and cold water for experiments that require it. There is a freezer in which you can prepare ice or cool substances to very low temperatures. The stove or oven allows you to heat or dry a wide variety of materials.

Your bathroom and kitchen together provide many useful chemicals that can be used in experiments, and, of course, your bathtub is an excellent place to immerse large objects, including your own body if you want to know how much space you take up. A stairwell is an excellent place to find out about falling objects. Your garage or basement probably contains a number of tools useful in building apparatus for experiments and for measuring results. Even the walls, ceilings, and floors of your house, as you will see, can help you explore science.

Of course, other members of your family are not going to be very happy if they stumble over your apparatus as they walk about the house. Thoughtful scientists do not let their work interfere with the activities of others. If your experiment must be conducted over a long period of time, try to set it up in a place that is out of the way of other people.

Do all your experiments with care. In some experiments you will need an older person to help you, or at least to stay nearby, to help you avoid injury.

Most of the experiments provide a lot of guidance. But some of them will raise questions and ask you to make up your own experiments to answer them. This is the kind of experiment that could be a particularly good start for a science fair project. Such experiments are marked with an asterisk (*).

As you do these experiments, you may discover new questions that you will be able to answer with experiments of your own design. By all means carry out these experiments (with your parents' permission). You are developing the kind of curiosity and ingenuity that is shared by all scientists.

1

BALANCES ARE FOR WEIGHING

In many experiments it is useful to have a balance to weigh things. You can build a simple balance of your own. But before you do, you might like to try some experiments that will help you understand how a balance works.

A balance, like any other device that turns, rotates about its center of gravity. To find out more about gravity, try Experiment 1.1.

Experiment 1.1

CENTER OF GRAVITY

To do this experiment you will need:

✔ ruler	✔ metal washer or nut
✔ stiff cardboard	✔ thread
✔ scissors	✔ pencil
✔ straight pin	

The center of gravity of anything is the point at which all the object's weight can be considered to be. It is the point about which the object has no tendency to rotate. It is therefore the point at which you can pick up the object without having it turn.

Try balancing a ruler on your fingertip in different ways: with a flat side, an edge, an end, or a corner resting on your fingertip. It will balance only if your fingertip is under the center of the ruler. In every position the ruler is difficult to balance, but you can see that the higher the center of the ruler is above your fingertip, the harder it is to balance.

Cut a sheet of stiff cardboard into an irregular shape. Where is the cardboard's center of gravity? One way to find out is to pin one end of the sheet to a basement wall or to a bulletin board, as shown in Figure 1. The cardboard should be free to swing on the pin. Now hang a plumb line from the pin. (You can make a plumb line—a line that points to the center of the earth—by tying a metal washer or nut to a piece of thread.) Draw a line beneath the thread along the cardboard sheet. The line marks the direction to the earth's center.

Now rotate the sheet through 60 to 90 degrees and again pin it at the top edge. Mark another line along the thread. Repeat several times. You will find that the lines all meet at

FIGURE 1

very nearly one point. This point is the center of gravity of the cardboard shape. To confirm that this point is the center of gravity, take the cardboard off the wall and place that point on your fingertip. Does the cardboard balance at the point you have marked? What happens if you try to balance the sheet at some other point?

Experiment 1.2

Your Center of Gravity

To do this experiment you will need:

✔ wooden block or   ✔ handkerchiefs
blackboard eraser
✔ weights

Where do you think your center of gravity is located? To find out, lean forward and balance your body on the back of a couch. At what point do you balance?

You can see how important it is to keep your center of gravity above your feet by doing the following experiment. Stand with the entire right side of your body, including the side of your right foot, in contact with a wall. Now try to lift your left foot. What happens? Does your body want to rotate about your center of gravity?

Now stand with your back against a wall. Be sure your heels are touching the wall. Drop a handkerchief just in front of your toes. Try to pick up the handkerchief without bending your knees or moving your feet. What happens when your center of gravity gets beyond your feet?

Do you think people's center of gravity will be different for boys than girls? Here is an experiment to find out.

Get down on your hands and knees and measure one *cubit* straight out from your knees, as shown in Figure 2. (A cubit is the length of your forearm from the elbow to the tip of your middle finger.) Place a wooden block or a blackboard eraser on its edge one cubit from your knees. With your hands behind your back, lean forward and try to knock the block over with your nose. Can you do it, or do you fall on your nose instead? Whether you can do it or not

FIGURE 2

wooden block
or
blackboard
eraser

← 1 cubit →

First measure distance, then place both hands behind back.

has nothing to do with how clever you are; it depends only on how you are built.

Have a number of different people try this experiment. Are girls generally more successful than boys?

As you lean forward, your center of gravity also moves forward. What will happen if your center of gravity gets out beyond your knees?

Repeat the experiment with some weights in your back pockets or tied to your calves with handkerchiefs. How will these weights change your center of gravity? Do they make it easier for you to tip the block over?

Do you see now why it is so hard to walk a tightrope or stand up in a small boat? Why is it dangerous to pull a chair away from someone who is in the process of sitting down?

Experiment 1.3

SOME STRANGE
BALANCING ACTS

To do this experiment you will need:

✔ large coin or washer	✔ table
✔ dinner forks	✔ thin cardboard or heavy paper
✔ soda bottle with cap	
✔ knife	✔ scissors
✔ apple or potato	✔ clear tape
✔ pencil	

You have seen how unstable an object (including your body) is when its center of gravity is above and beyond its point of support. However, if the center of gravity of an object is below its point of support, it will not tip over. You can see this for yourself by building some strange balancing acts.

Insert a large coin or washer between the two upper tines of a pair of forks (see Figure 3). You will find you can balance the connected objects on the top of a capped soda bottle. What

FIGURE 3

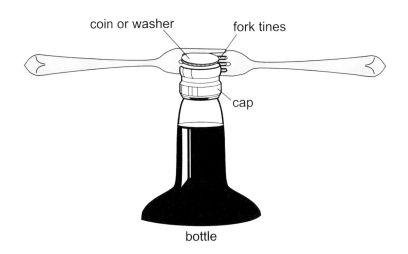

happens if you try this balancing act with the coin between the two lowest tines? Why?

Cut a large slice of apple or potato approximately one inch thick. Carefully push a pencil through the slice and insert a fork below the pencil, as shown in Figure 4. Balance the object on the edge of a table. If you want, you can make a small cardboard silhouette and tape it to the end of the pencil. A slight downward push on the pencil will provide a dancing silhouette.

With two forks in the slice, you can balance the slice with the pencil upright, as shown in Figure 5. Turn the cardboard figure

FIGURE 4

90 degrees and give the pencil a gentle twirl if you want to see your dancer do a pirouette.

Now that you know the secret of strange balancing acts, try making some of your own.

Figure 5

Experiment 1.4*

A SODA STRAW BALANCE

To do this experiment you will need:

✔ pin or needle

✔ soda straw

✔ supports; e.g., cans, glasses, books

✔ paper clips

Place the ends of a pin or needle on two supports, such as two cans, glasses, or books. Try to balance a soda straw on the pin. Why is it so hard to do?

Now see if you can balance the straw by pushing the pin or needle through the straw, as shown in Figure 6a. When you succeed, look at the position of the pin. Is it near the middle or near one end of the straw? How about its position from top to bottom of the straw? In which of the three positions shown in Figure 6b is the straw easiest to balance? Why do you think that is the easiest balancing position? *Hint:* Where is the straw's center of gravity?

Will the straw remain balanced if you turn it end for end? If you turn it top for bottom?

FIGURE 6

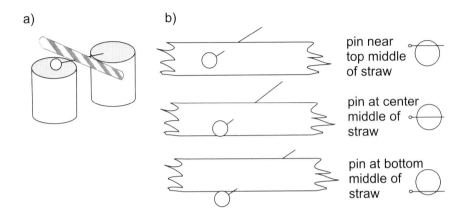

Hang a paper clip over one end of the balanced straw. (If the clip slides along the straw, you may have to pinch the sides of the clip so that they rub against the straw.) How can you make the straw balance again without removing the paper clip?

Figure 7a shows just one half of a balanced soda straw. There are clips on the other half, too. What must the other half of the straw look like in each case?

Figure 7b contains more drawings of the left halves of some balanced soda straws. What must the right half of the straw look like if it has only *one* paper clip on it?

FIGURE 7

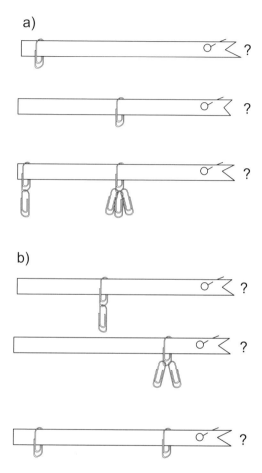

Where would you place two paper clips on the left half of the straw so that it would be impossible to balance the straw with only one paper clip on the right half? Could you make it balance if you moved the pin that supports the straw at its center?

Experiment 1.5*

BUILDING A BALANCE

To do this experiment you will need:

- ✔ ruler
- ✔ rigid cardboard
- ✔ pencil
- ✔ sharp shears or knife and an ADULT
- ✔ finishing nail
- ✔ supports; e.g., cans, glasses, books
- ✔ 10 paper clips
- ✔ 12 identical metal washers
- ✔ small Styrofoam or aluminum cups
- ✔ string or pipe cleaners
- ✔ clay
- ✔ water
- ✔ eyedropper
- ✔ coins for weighing

Place a ruler on a sheet of stiff cardboard. Draw an outline of the ruler with a pencil. Use sharp shears (or **ask an adult** to use a sharp knife) to cut out the cardboard section you have marked. Draw a straight line across the width of the cardboard rectangle at its exact center. Draw similar lines at one-inch intervals to both the right and left side of the center line. Then draw a line parallel to the length of the cardboard ¼ inch from the edge.

Use a small finishing nail to punch the holes shown in Figure 8.

FIGURE 8

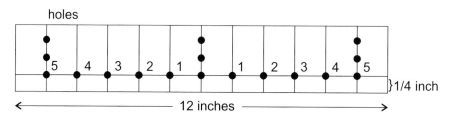

Push the nail through the top center hole. Support the ends of the nail with two empty cans, glasses, or books. Unbend ten identical paper clips into hook shapes. Hang them from the ten holes that are one inch apart along the cardboard beam, as shown in Figure 9a. If the beam is not level, use scissors to trim a little off the heavy end. Before you finish making your balance, take a few minutes to figure out how it works.

Find about a dozen identical steel washers. Hang one washer on the clip at the number 5 position. Where can you hang a second washer to make the beam level again? Where should you place a single washer on the left side of the beam to balance two washers at the number 2 position on the right side?

FIGURE 9

a)

b)

Try a variety of combination of washers and positions that make the balance beam level. Record your results. Then see if you can predict the numbers that belong in the blank spaces in Table 1 to make the beam balance. Can you find a rule that enables you to predict when the weights at various positions will balance?

TABLE 1

PREDICTING BALANCING POSITIONS

Test	Left side		Right side	
	Number of Washers	at position	Number of Washers	at position
A	2	5	2	5
B	2	2	1	4
C	5	3	3	—
D	3	—	—	—
E	1 and 2	4 and 3	2 and —	— and —
F	2 and 3	5 and 2	— and 1	3 and 4

From your experiments you can see that in achieving balance, the distance of the weights from the center of the beam is just as important as the number of weights. Have you found a rule yet that allows you to predict whether the beam will balance? If not, see if you can find a way to make the number of washers and their distances from the beam's center equal for both the right and the left sides of the beam. Try adding, dividing, or multiplying the number of washers and distances from the center each time the beam is balanced.

You might enjoy playing a balance game. Place some washers at different places on one side of the beam. Challenge a friend to make the beam balance by placing washers on the other side. He or she may place the washers at more than one place, but the washers may not be moved once they have been placed on the hooks. Then it is your friend's turn to challenge you.

You have probably found that if the number of washers multiplied by their distance from the center of the beam is the same on both the right and the left sides of the beam, then the beam will balance. That is why most balances are built so that you place the known and unknown weight at equal distances from the center of the beam.

But there is much more to learn about balances. For example, does it make a difference where you place the nail that supports the center of the beam? To find out, remove all the paper clips except the two in the number 5 holes. Make two pans for your balance using small cups and string or pipe cleaners. Hang the cups from the two paper clips at each end of the beam, as shown in Figure 9b. If the beam is not level, trim a little cardboard from its heavy end or add clay to the light side.

To test the effect of the position of the nail at the center of the beam, you can use water drops as a unit of weight. (You can add the water with an eyedropper.) With the nail through the upper hole at the beam's center, how many drops of water must you add to one pan before it touches the table? Now dry the pan and repeat the experiment with the nail through the center hole. What happens if you repeat the experiment with the nail through the lowest hole?

With the nail through the top hole, tipping the balance to the right moves the beam's center of gravity to the left side of the line that runs from the support pin to the center of the

FIGURE 10

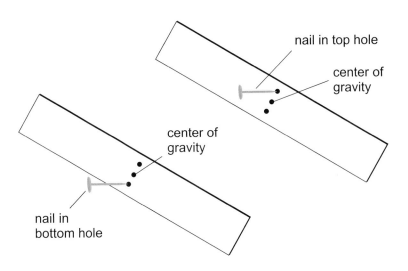

nail in top hole

center of gravity

center of gravity

nail in bottom hole

earth. This makes the beam swing back toward its original position, as you can see in Figure 10.

If the nail is through the bottom hole, tipping the beam to the right moves the beam's center of gravity to the right, too. This causes the beam to continue turning to the right.

As you have seen, the balance is very stable (well balanced) when the nail is through the top hole. However, it is not very sensitive; that is, it does not move very far when a small amount of weight is added to one side. If the nail is through the bottom hole, the balance is so sensitive that it is useless; it just swings all the way to the heavy side.

Put the nail through the center hole. Now test the stability and sensitivity of the balance when the *pans* are suspended from the top, middle, and lower holes at the ends of the beam. Which arrangement is most sensitive? Which is unstable? Which is least sensitive?

What will happen to the sensitivity of your balance if you move the pans closer to the center of the beam?

If you place several washers in each pan, will it affect the sensitivity of the balance?

How could you build a better balance?

Now use your balance to weigh some things. Which is heavier, a penny or a dime? A nickel or two dimes?

If you have identical paper clips, you can use them as a unit of weight. For example, how many paper clips does a penny weigh? How about a washer? How could you weigh something that weighs less than a paper clip? How could you weigh something that weighs between three and four paper clips?

2
WEIGHING IN THE KITCHEN

You know how to build a balance and use it to weigh things. But you can use a balance to do other things as well. You can compare the "stickiness" of different liquids or find out how much water is in a certain food by using a balance. A balance will help you to find the compactness (density) of different substances; however, you can often determine which of several substances is most or least compact without a balance.

Experiment 2.1*

HOW STICKY ARE DIFFERENT LIQUIDS?

To do this experiment you will need:

✔ balance	✔ water
✔ ruler	✔ flat container of water
✔ plastic lid	✔ paper clips
✔ sharp scissors	✔ soap
✔ straight pin	✔ rubbing alcohol
✔ pliers	✔ cooking oil
✔ string	✔ towel

You can measure the stickiness or "hold-togetherness" of various liquids by measuring how much pull (in paper clips) is required to pull the liquid apart. To measure the pull, you can use the balance you built, but first you will need to make a plate that will adhere to liquids. That is easy to do. Just cut a 5-cm (2-in) square from a plastic cover such as the ones found on coffee cans, margarine tubs, and artificial whipped topping containers. Push a straight pin through the center of the square.

If you find this difficult, **ask an adult** to help you heat the end of the pin with a match while you hold it with pliers. The hot pin will then go through the plastic very easily. Use the pliers to bend the sharp end of the pin into a loop so that you can hang it from one end of the balance with string or a paper clip, as shown in Figure 11. If the beam is not level, add a little clay to one side of the beam, or slide an opened paper clip along the light side of the beam until it is level.

Once the beam is level, place the plastic square on the surface of some tap water in a clean container. How many paper clips, gently

FIGURE 11

placed in the cup on the other side of the beam, are required to pull the water apart? (If you look closely, you will see that there is water on the plastic plate. This shows that the water pulled apart.) Repeat the experiment again to see if you get similar results. If you need fractions of a paper clip, you can hang an opened paper clip on the beam and slide it from the center outward until the beam is level. Since the beam is divided into fifths, each fifth you slide the clip is equal to 0.2 paper clip. Halfway between the third and fourth is equivalent to 0.7 paper clip.

Add some soap to the water. Does soapy water pull apart more easily than plain water?

Try to pull apart other liquids, such as rubbing alcohol and cooking oil. Be sure to clean and dry the plate and the container that holds the liquid before each experiment.

Will the shape of the plate affect the results of your experiment? How about the surface area of the plate? When you change the shape of the plate, what should you do about the surface area? Do experiments to answer these questions. What do you find?

Experiment 2.2

THE PAPER TOWEL SOAK-UP

To do this experiment you will need:

✔ paper towels   ✔ paper clips
✔ balance   ✔ a nickel

Remove the pans from your balance and hang half a paper towel on the paper clip hook at the left end of the beam. Hang paper clips on the other end in order to find the weight of the towel. How many paper clips does the half-towel weigh? Now wet the towel. When the excess water has dripped off, weigh the wet towel. How much water, in paper clips, did the towel absorb?

To find the weight in grams, you need to know the weight of a paper clip in grams. You can find out very easily by using paper clips to weigh a nickel. A nickel weighs 5 grams. How many grams of water did the paper towel absorb?

Watch the balance beam as the towel dries. How long does it take for the towel to lose a paper clip's weight of water? What can you do to make the towel dry faster?

Experiment 2.3*

DENSITY: A MEASURE OF COMPACTNESS

To do this experiment you will need:

✔ balance	✔ rubbing alcohol
✔ paper clips	✔ salt
✔ small wood block	✔ water
✔ clay	✔ cooking oil
✔ medicine cups	

A piece of gold weighs more than seven times as much as a piece of aluminum of the same size (volume). This tells you that gold is much more compact than aluminum. Scientists say that gold is *denser* than aluminum. If you divide the weight of anything by its volume, the number you get is called the density of that material. For example, a cubic foot of water weighs 62.4 pounds. Therefore, its density is 62.4 pounds per cubic foot. One cubic centimeter of gold weighs 19.3 grams; its density is 19.3 g/cm^3.

You can find out which of two materials is denser by placing equal volumes of the two substances on opposite sides of an equal-arm balance. Try it with a wooden block and a piece of clay that you have made equal in size and shape to the wood. Which block is denser?

If you change the shape of the clay block, will its density change? How can you check the accuracy of your prediction?

With a medicine cup you can compare the weights of equal volumes of different liquids. Is rubbing alcohol more or less dense than water? How about cooking oil? Salt water?

How could you measure the actual densities of these liquids in grams per cubic centimeter (g/cm^3) or grams per milliliter (g/ml)? (A milliliter and a cubic centimeter are the same volume.)

Experiment 2.4

DROPS AND DENSITIES

To do this experiment you will need:

- ✔ hot water
- ✔ cold water
- ✔ food coloring
- ✔ eyedropper
- ✔ drinking glasses or jars

- ✔ tablespoon
- ✔ salt (preferably kosher)
- ✔ vials (pill bottles)
- ✔ various liquids and solids

There is another way to compare the densities of liquids. What do you think will happen if you *slowly* squeeze a drop of cooking oil from the end of an eyedropper into the middle of a container of water? Will the drop go up or down, or will it remain in the middle? What will happen if you squeeze a drop of water into the center of some cooking oil?

The drop test is a very sensitive way to compare densities. To see this for yourself, use a drop of food coloring to color some hot tap water. Now slowly squeeze a drop of the hot colored water into a container of cold tap water, as shown in Figure 12. What does your experiment tell you about the density of hot water as compared with that of cold water?

Repeat the experiment, but this time color the cold water and squeeze a drop of it into some hot water. What do you predict will happen to the drop?

Try the test with liquids that differ only slightly in density. Fill four identical glasses three-fourths full of tap water. Add one tablespoonful of salt to the first glass of water. (If possible, use kosher salt; it makes a clear

FIGURE 12

hot water

vial

cold water

solution because it has no additives.) Add two tablespoonfuls to the second glass, and three to the third. Stir all three liquids until the salt is dissolved. Add several drops of food coloring to each liquid. You might color one liquid red, another blue, and the third green. The fourth, the unsalted water, can be left uncolored.

To determine the density order of the four liquids, from least dense to most dense, put samples of the four liquids into separate pill bottles or vials and, using an eyedropper, add drops of one to the others. How many combinations are there to try? Which test, balance or drop, do you think is more sensitive?

In addition to the three salt solutions and water, you might like to test some other liquids and add them to your density list. You could try rubbing alcohol, cooking oil, sugar water, apple juice, milk, and many other liquids.

You could also add solids to your list. Are all solids denser than all liquids? How about wood? Clay? Aluminum? Other solids? Where does each solid fit into your density order?

Experiment 2.5*

How Much of the Food You Eat Is Water?

To do this experiment you will need:

✔ various kinds of food	✔ small aluminum pans
✔ balance	✔ oven
✔ paper clips	✔ pencil and paper

Take some small pieces of different foods: bread, potato, carrot, celery, and cereal. Weigh each food and record your results. Place the foods in separate small aluminum pans. Put the pans in a warm oven for several hours to dry. Weigh the food again and continue heating and weighing until there is no further weight change. Record the dry weight of each food piece. Then calculate what percentage of the food was water. For example, if a piece of bread weighed 6 paper clips before drying and 2 paper clips afterward, its water content was 4 paper clips. Thus, the water made up four-sixths, or about 67 percent, of the bread.

Which of the foods you tested contains the largest percentage of water? Which food was the driest?

Experiment 2.6

SOME DENSITY INVESTIGATIONS

To do this experiment you will need:

- ✔ balloons
- ✔ tie bands
- ✔ balance
- ✔ Alka-Seltzer antacid tablets
- ✔ water
- ✔ soda bottle
- ✔ tire pump
- ✔ stone
- ✔ steel washers
- ✔ container
- ✔ various metals
- ✔ clay
- ✔ bathtub
- ✔ soap

As you might guess, gases have very low densities. But do all gases have the same density? To find out, get two identical balloons and tie bands. Use the tie bands to hang the balloons from opposite ends of your balance. Be sure the beam is level.

Prepare some carbon dioxide gas by breaking three or four Alka-Seltzer tablets into small pieces and adding them to about an inch of water in a small soda bottle. Attach a balloon to the neck of the bottle to collect the carbon dioxide. When the reaction between water and Alka-Seltzer is over (the bubbles will stop), carefully remove the balloon. Use a tie band to seal the balloon and hang it from the same end of the balance where it was before. Use a tire pump to put an equal volume of air in another identical balloon. Close it off with a tie band. Use the balance to see if one gas is denser than the other.

Replace the pump air in one balloon with your own lung air. Which is denser, lung air or carbon dioxide? Lung air or pump air? Is the air that you exhale pure carbon dioxide? How do you know?

Which is denser, a stone or steel washers? To find out you will need to determine the weight per volume for each solid, or compare the weights of equal volumes. (*Hint:* An object that sinks in water displaces a volume of water equal to its own volume.)

Use the same method to compare, or actually measure, the densities of steel, aluminum, copper, brass, and lead.

You have seen that both clay and steel sink in water. This tells you these solids are denser than water, yet steel ships float. Even the concrete boats used in World War II floated. If you can make a piece of clay float, you will probably be able to explain why steel or concrete boats float. Try it. Can you explain why even boats made of concrete can be made to float?

Next time you go swimming, try to float on the surface on your back. What happens to your position in the water when you inhale a deep breath? What happens when you exhale? How do you explain your observations?

Which is densest, you, your bath soap, or your bath water? Which is least dense? How do you know?

Experiment 2.7*

How Much Does Air Weigh?

To do this experiment you will need:

✔ tie bands	✔ balance
✔ plastic bag	✔ paper clips

Use a tie band to hang an empty plastic bag from one end of your balance. How much does the bag weigh? Swing the bag swiftly through the air as you hold it open. Use the same tie band to close off the air trapped in the bag. Then weigh the bag and the air. How much does the air appear to weigh? Are you surprised by your results?

To help you understand why air appears to be weightless, try the next two experiments.

Experiment 2.8

WEIGHING WATER IN WATER

To do this experiment you will need:

✔ balance	✔ tie band
✔ balloon	✔ jar
✔ water	✔ salt (preferably kosher)
✔ pitcher or measuring cup	✔ rubbing alcohol

After you have leveled your balance beam, carefully fill a balloon with water. Let the bottom of the balloon rest on the kitchen counter as you slowly pour in tap water from a small pitcher or measuring cup. Wait a few moments for air bubbles to leave. Then tie off the balloon with a tie band, being careful not to form any air pockets in the balloon. Hang the water balloon from one end of the balance. Place a large jar of water beneath the balloon and raise it until the balloon is submerged. You will find that the water balloon now appears to be weightless. In fact, if you were careful not to get any air bubbles in the balloon, the water-filled balloon will neither sink nor float when released in the jar.

What happens when you place the water balloon in a jar of salt water? In a jar of rubbing alcohol? In what gas did you weigh air?

Experiment 2.9

WEIGHING SOLIDS IN LIQUIDS

To do this experiment you will need:

✔ clay or metal washer ✔ jar

✔ tie band ✔ water

✔ balance ✔ salt

✔ paper clips ✔ rubbing alcohol

Weigh a piece of clay or a metal washer by attaching it to one end of your balance with a tie band. Then reweigh the solid while it is submerged in a jar of water. What happens to the apparent weight of the solid?

Do you think the solid will appear to weigh more or will it appear to weigh less if weighed in salt water? If weighed in rubbing alcohol? Test your predictions with an experiment.

Would carbon dioxide appear to weigh more in air or in a vacuum? How much do you think carbon dioxide would appear to weigh in an atmosphere of carbon dioxide?

3
HOT AND COLD AND WET

You have already seen that much of the food we eat is really water. Now you will discover how water becomes rain and fog. You will find also that even on a clear day there is water all around us.

Experiment 3.1

FOG AND HUMIDITY

To do this experiment you will need:

✔ jar	✔ warm water
✔ ice	✔ shiny metal can
✔ hot water	✔ spoon for stirring
✔ thin plastic bag	

Find a jar with a mouth slightly smaller than the size of an ice cube. Fill the jar with *hot* water; then pour out all but about an inch of the water. Place an ice cube on the mouth of the jar and hold the jar up to the light. Do you see thin streams of fog forming where the warm air in the jar meets the ice?

Where did the fog come from, the ice or the warm air? Repeat the experiment, but this time wrap the ice cube in a small, thin plastic bag.

The fact that fog still forms shows that the moisture did not come from the ice. It must have come from the warm air above the hot water.

Just as sugar dissolves in water and cannot be seen, so water dissolves in air. And, like particles of sugar, the particles of water are so small they cannot be seen. You may know that more sugar will dissolve in hot water than in cold water. Perhaps more water can dissolve in hot air than in cold air.

At any temperature there is a limit to the amount of sugar that will dissolve in a liter of water. When this limit is reached, we say the solution is saturated. If the temperature of a saturated sugar solution decreases, the water cannot hold as much sugar. The sugar in excess of saturation falls out of solution. Is the same true of water in the atmosphere?

To test this idea, slowly lower the temperature of some warm water in a *shiny* metal can. You can do this by adding small pieces of ice to the water as you stir it. If our idea is correct, water should fall out of the air (condense) when the air is cold enough to form a saturated solution of water in air. Look for signs of moisture on the outside of the can as the temperature falls. Can you find evidence to support our idea?

In the summertime you have probably seen moisture on the *outside* of a cold pitcher of iced tea or milk. How do you explain such moisture? Where have you seen condensed moisture in the wintertime?

Experiment 3.2*

Absolute Humidity

To do this experiment you will need:

✔ thermometer

✔ jar

✔ ice

✔ hot water

✔ thin plastic bag

✔ warm water

✔ shiny metal can

✔ spoon for stirring

The water dissolved in air is called humidity. The quantity of water dissolved in one cubic meter of air is called the absolute humidity. It can be measured using a method similar to the one you used in the previous experiment. Just repeat that experiment, but this time stir the water with a thermometer as you cool it. Record the temperature at which you first see moisture condensing on the can. This temperature is called the dew point.

Once you have found the dew point, you can use Table 2 to determine the absolute humidity. The table gives the maximum amount of water that can be dissolved in one cubic meter of air at a given temperature. You know the dew point; therefore you know the temperature at which the air in contact with the can is saturated with water vapor. For example, suppose the air in the room you are working in is 20°C (68°F), and you find the dew point to be 10°C (50°F). From the table you see that the air holds 9.3 g/m^3.

At 20°C (68°F) the air could hold 17.1 grams of moisture per cubic meter. But in our example it contains only 9.3 grams of the 17.1 grams it could hold. Therefore, it contains only 9.3/17.1 or 54 percent of the moisture required for saturation. This ratio—the water vapor present in the air compared to the total vapor the air could hold if saturated—when expressed as a percentage, is called the relative humidity.

TABLE 2

GRAMS OF MOISTURE IN ONE CUBIC METER OF SATURATED AIR AT VARIOUS TEMPERATURES

Temperature	Water Vapor (grams)	Temperature	Water Vapor (grams)
0°C (32°F)	4.8	20°C (68°F)	17.1
5°C (41°F)	6.8	25°C (77°F)	22.8
10°C (50°F)	9.3	30°C (86°F)	30.0
15°C (59°F)	12.7	35°C (95°F)	39.2

Use the dew point and the temperature of the air to determine the absolute and relative humidity in your kitchen. Repeat the experiment in your bathroom just after you take a shower. Which room do you think will have the greatest *absolute* humidity? The greatest *relative* humidity?

Try the same experiment in various parts of your house and outdoors. Try it on clear, cloudy, and rainy days. Try it at different times of the year. What changes in absolute and relative humidity do you find?

Experiment 3.3*

EVAPORATION

To do this experiment you will need:

✔ water	✔ marking pen
✔ 5 drinking glasses	✔ small plate or saucer
✔ masking tape	✔ electric fan

Most of the moisture in air comes from lakes and oceans through a process called evaporation. To see what evaporation is, fill five identical drinking glasses about three-fourths full of water. Line the glasses up and be sure they all contain the same volume. Using masking tape and a marking pen, make a mark on each glass at the water level.

Put one glass in a warm, open place (on a radiator might be a good location). Put another in a cool but not freezing open place (near a window in the wintertime would be good). Leave the third one at room temperature. Place the fourth near the third, but cover it with a small plate or saucer. The fifth glass should be placed in front of an electric fan if you have one.

Mark the water levels in each glass over a period of several days. Which glass seemed to lose the most water? Which one lost none? What effect did temperature have on the water lost?

The escape of water from its surface is called evaporation. Where do you think the water goes? What was the purpose of the covered glass in this experiment?

Experiment 3.4

EVAPORATION IS COOL

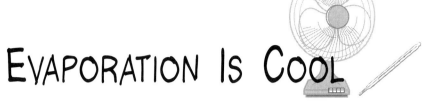

To do this experiment you will need:

✔ thermometer	✔ thin cloth
✔ electric fan	✔ water

On a hot summer day, what can you do to cool off if you do not have an air conditioner?

Outside you might look for a place where there is a breeze; indoors you might turn on a fan. In a moving car you could open a window and let the air flow over you. All these ways of getting cool involve moving air. Is moving air really cooler than still air?

To find out, place a thermometer in a room. After a few minutes record the temperature. Now place a fan in front of the thermometer. Does the temperature go up, down, or remain the same? Is moving air cooler than still air?

Swimming is another way to get cool. In fact, when you come out of the water and stand in a breeze, you may feel cold and start to shiver. You know the moving air is not cold; cooling off must have something to do with your wet skin. Could the evaporation of water from your skin make you feel cold?

You know from the previous experiment that water evaporates faster when air is moving over it.

To see if rapid evaporation can cool a moist object, soak a strip of thin cloth in water. Wrap the cloth around the bulb of a thermometer. When the liquid in the thermometer tube stops moving, note the temperature. Then hold the thermometer in front of a spinning fan or swing it through the air for a few minutes. What happens to the temperature?

Evaporation happens because the fastest-moving molecules in a liquid are constantly leaving the surface to become a gas. When water evaporates, it becomes the gas—the water vapor—that makes up the humidity in the air. Because the fastest-moving molecules are the warmest ones, the ones that remain behind in the liquid are the cooler ones; hence the liquid becomes cooler as it evaporates.

Experiment 3.5

COOLING AND THE RATE OF EVAPORATION

To do this experiment you will need:

✔ hot water	✔ 3 thermometers
✔ 3 aluminum pie pans	✔ cooking oil
✔ newspaper	✔ electric fan

Knowing that a liquid cools as it evaporates, try to predict how the *rate* of evaporation will affect the temperature of an evaporating liquid.

To check your prediction, pour equal amounts of hot water into three identical aluminum pie pans. Place the pans on folded newspapers for insulation. Submerge a thermometer in each pan. To keep the evaporation rate near zero in one pan, add a few drops of cooking oil to cover the water. Leave a second pan undisturbed. To increase the rate of evaporation in a third pan, use an electric fan to blow air across it, but make sure the air from the fan does not go near the other two pans.

Record the temperature in each pan at one-minute intervals for a few minutes. In which pan does the water cool fastest? Did you predict correctly?

Can you explain why sweating keeps you cool?

Experiment 3.6

RAIN IN THE KITCHEN

To do this experiment you will need:

✔ an ADULT	✔ pan
✔ teakettle	✔ ice water
✔ stove	✔ water
✔ oven mitt	

You have seen that warm air holds more moisture than cold air. You have seen also that when the temperature falls below the dew point, water vapor in the air begins to fall out of solution.

Using these principles, you can make it rain in your kitchen. **Under adult supervision**, heat a teakettle of water to boiling on the kitchen stove. (**Be careful using the stove. Be sure to turn it off when you are finished.**) Using an oven mitt, hold a pan of ice in the stream of steam emerging from the teakettle. Can you make it "rain" from the bottom of the cold pan?

Experiment 3.7

MAKE A CLOUD

To do this experiment you will need:

- ✔ cold water
- ✔ glass bottle
- ✔ an ADULT
- ✔ wooden matches
- ✔ air pump
- ✔ one-hole rubber stopper
- ✔ safety glasses
- ✔ thermometer

The formation of rain droplets in the atmosphere is more complex than the "kitchen rain" you produced. Tiny droplets of rain form on minute particles of salt or dust that serve as condensation nuclei. And the water vapor is cooled by its expansion as it ascends into the upper atmosphere, where the pressure is less.

You can see this effect for yourself. Put some cold water in a clear glass bottle. *Be sure the bottle has no cracks.* Shake the bottle with your hand over its mouth to saturate the enclosed air with water vapor. **Have an adult** blow out a burning match and let the smoke escape into the mouth of the inverted bottle. The smoke particles will serve as condensation nuclei so that droplets of water can form as the water vapor cools. To cool the air and vapor, connect an air pump to a one-hole rubber stopper and put the stopper into the bottle's mouth. **Put on safety glasses now.** Pump air into the bottle until you pop the stopper. The expansion of the pressurized air will cool the vapor, causing it to condense into tiny droplets that form a cloud inside the bottle.

Just as expansion causes a gas to cool, so compression will cause a gas to become warmer. To see this effect, use an air pump to force compressed air across the bulb of a thermometer. What happens to the temperature?

In a diesel engine the compression of the fuel vapor produces a temperature high enough to ignite the vapor. As a result, diesel engines, unlike gasoline engines, do not have spark plugs.

Experiment 3.8

AIR PRESSURE

To do this experiment you will need:

✔ pail or sink	✔ one-gallon metal can with cap or rubber stopper to fit opening
✔ water	
✔ water glass	✔ stove
✔ index card	✔ pot holders or oven mitts
✔ an ADULT	✔ cardboard sheet or heatproof mat

To see that air really does exert a pressure, try these experiments.

Fill a pail or sink with water. Submerge a drinking glass and fill it. Turn the glass under water so that it is upside down, and slowly lift it until most of it, but not the open end, is out of the water. As you can see, the water in the glass is well above the water level in the sink. Normally, gravity would cause water to fall from the glass. What is keeping the water up?

Fill a glass to the brim with water. Place an index card on the glass. Put your hand on top of the card and invert the glass of water over the sink. Remove your hand. Why doesn't the card fall from the glass and the water spill out?

Here is an even more dramatic experiment to show the presence of air pressure. In this experiment you will get rid of the air that is normally inside a container. Then you will be able to see the effect of the force that air pressure exerts when there is little or no opposing force.

Ask an adult to help you with this experiment; he or she will enjoy it as much as you will.

Take a one-gallon metal can like the ones that paint thinner and olive oil come in. If the can's screw-on cap is missing, use a rubber stopper that fits the opening in the can.

Rinse the can thoroughly to remove any flammable liquid that might remain. Pour a cup of water into the can. Leave the top of the can open and heat the can on the stove. Steam from the boiling water will drive air out of the can. Let the water boil for several minutes to be sure that most of the air is gone.

Using oven mitts or pot holders to protect your hands, remove the can from the heat and place it on a thick piece of cardboard or a heatproof mat. *Immediately* seal the can with its screw-on cap or a rubber stopper.

As the can cools, the steam will condense, leaving the can very nearly empty. Watch how the air outside the can, unopposed now by air that is normally inside, pushes inward on all sides of the can. You will be amazed by the strength of air!

How Far Away Is the Storm?

To do this experiment you will need:

✔ watch or clock with a
  second hand

You probably know that thunder is caused by the expansion of air heated by a lightning stroke. But the speed of sound ($^1/_5$ mile per second or 331 meters per second) is negligible compared with the speed of light (186,000 miles per second or 300,000 kilometers per second). That is why you see the lightning before you hear the thunder.

Because the light from lightning reaches your eyes almost instantaneously, you can use the time delay between the sight of lightning and the sound of the thunder it creates to determine how far away the lightning was. Count the number of seconds between the lightning and the thunder. Since sound travels $^1/_5$ mile per second or $^1/_3$ kilometer per second, it takes 5 seconds to go one mile and 3 seconds to go one kilometer. If you divide the number of seconds between lightning and thunder by 5, you will have the distance to the lightning in miles. How would you find the distance in kilometers?

Repeat the experiment every few minutes. Is the storm approaching or moving away?

4
From Ceiling to Floor: The Science of Falling Objects

It was Galileo, in the sixteenth century, who first studied falling bodies scientifically—that is, by doing experiments with falling things, not just talking about them.

You, too, can experiment with falling objects. But be careful that you do not fall with them.

Experiment 4.1

DIFFERENT WEIGHT, DIFFERENT FALL?

To do this experiment you will need:

✔ several balls of different weight; e.g., tennis ball, baseball, lacrosse ball

✔ paper

✔ book

Hold a heavy ball and a light ball at the same height. Predict which will hit the floor first if you release both of them at the same time. Repeat the experiment several times. Galileo found that objects with different weights fall together. Do you agree? Drop the two balls at the same time from various equal heights. Do they still fall side by side?

Now drop a ball and a piece of paper from the same height at the same time. Do they fall together?

Repeat the experiment, but this time crumple the paper into a tight ball. What do you find about their falling rates now?

Place a sheet of paper on the cover of a book that is larger than the paper, as shown in

Figure 13. Drop the book and paper. Why do they fall together?

Galileo guessed that the small force between the air and a light piece of paper would be enough to cause the paper to fall more slowly than a much heavier object. But, he argued, in a vacuum both paper and ball would fall together. Years later, when scientists were able to make a vacuum, a coin and a feather were found to fall side by side.

During a moon walk, American astronauts tested Galileo's hypothesis by dropping a hammer and a feather. In the airless space above the moon's surface, the two objects fell at the same rate, just as Galileo predicted they would.

FIGURE 13

paper

book

Experiment 4.2*

THE SPEED OF A FALLING BALL

To do this experiment you will need:

✔ ball	✔ yardstick or meterstick

If you count from one to five as fast as you can, you will find it takes just about one second. Try it ten times in a row and you will see that just about ten seconds have elapsed.

You can use this method of timing to estimate fractions of a second. For example, if you start counting as fast as you can when an event begins and you have counted to three when the event ends, then the event took approximately 3/5 (0.6) of a second.

Drop a ball from a height of one yard or one meter. At the moment you release the ball, begin counting as fast as you can. Stop counting when the ball hits the floor. Repeat the experiment several times until you are quite sure how long it takes the ball to fall. You will find it is just over 0.4 seconds; that is, you will be just starting to say "three" when the ball hits the floor.

How far will the ball have to travel to make its fall take twice as long—about 0.9 second? Does a height of 2 yards or meters work? If it did, what would it tell you about the ball's falling speed?

After doing an experiment similar to the one you have just tried, Galileo was convinced that falling objects do not travel at constant speed. He also realized, as you probably have, that the time intervals required for objects to fall small distances were too small to measure accurately. To overcome this difficulty he devised an ingenious means of diluting gravity. Using this device, he found that a ball had to fall 4 meters to take twice the time required to fall 1 meter. Do you agree?

Experiment 4.3*

DILUTING GRAVITY

To do this experiment you will need:

- ✔ heavy toy truck
- ✔ spring scale or long rubber band or a chain of short rubber bands
- ✔ smooth board
- ✔ 2 yardsticks or metersticks
- ✔ book or block
- ✔ pieces of wood or metal for separating yardsticks
- ✔ a large marble
- ✔ stopwatch (optional)

Galileo believed that bodies fall toward the earth because of a force we call gravity—an attraction that earth has for all matter. No one knows why there is such a force. There are certainly no strings or ropes connecting you or any object to the center of the earth; yet the force is there and we all feel it.

To dilute the force of gravity Galileo built an inclined plane. You can see for yourself that the force of gravity is diluted by such a plane. Hang a heavy toy truck from a spring scale, a long rubber band, or a chain of short rubber bands hooked together. Determine how much the spring or rubber is stretched by the weight of the truck. Then place the truck against a long board and slowly lower the board from a vertical toward a horizontal position, thus making it an inclined place (see Figure 14). What happens to the force needed to move the truck along the board as the angle between the board and the floor becomes smaller? Do you see why Galileo thought of an inclined plane as a way of diluting the force of gravity?

To see how much easier it is to measure time when gravity is diluted, build the inclined plane shown in Figure 15 using two yardsticks or metersticks and a book or block. Separate the sticks with small pieces of wood or metal

FIGURE 14

FIGURE 15

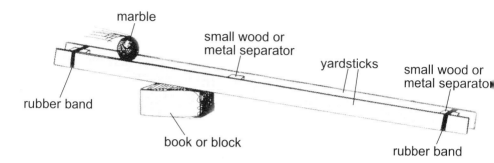

marble

small wood or metal separator

yardsticks

small wood or metal separato▮

rubber band

book or block

rubber band

so that a large marble will roll easily down the incline when one end is raised about 5 cm (2 in) above the floor or counter.

How long does it take the marble to roll from the 5-cm (2-in) line to the 25-cm (10-in) line, a distance of 20 cm (8 in)? You can time the descent with a stopwatch or by counting to five very fast as you did before. According to Galileo, how long should it take the marble to roll 81 cm (32 in), from the 5-cm (2-in) line to the 86-cm (34-in) line? Try it. How long did it take? What was the average speed of the marble, in centimeters or inches per second, while it was rolling the first 20 cm (8 in)? What was its average speed for 81 cm (32 in)? What is happening to the speed of the marble as it "falls" along the incline?

Experiment 4.4*

WHAT IS YOUR REACTION TIME?

To do this experiment you will need:

✔ dollar bill	✔ yardstick or meterstick

Offer to let your friends keep a dollar if they can catch it before it falls through their fingers. It is quite certain that you will keep your dollar. A dollar is about 15 cm (6 in) long. Have the person trying to catch the bill hold his or her thumb and index finger about 5 cm (2 in) above the bottom edge of the bill before you release it. Your friend must react before the dollar falls 10 cm (4 in)—a period of only 0.15 second. Few people, if any, can see the bill start to fall and then react fast enough to catch it.

To test someone's reaction time, have that person place his or her fingers loosely around the bottom of a yardstick that you hold in a vertical position. Tell the person to catch the yardstick as quickly as possible after it starts to fall.

From Table 3, you can determine the person's reaction time.

TABLE 3

REACTION TIMES ON THE BASIS OF THE DISTANCE A YARDSTICK FALLS BEFORE BEING CAUGHT

If the yardstick falls this distance, in inches, before being caught . . .	the person's reaction time, in seconds, is
6	0.177
12	0.250
18	0.306
24	0.353
30	0.395
36	0.433

Experiment 4.5

FALLING SIDEWAYS

To do this experiment you will need:

- ✔ metal washers
- ✔ string or thread
- ✔ tongue depressor, paper clips, or Popsicle stick
- ✔ tape
- ✔ yardstick or meterstick
- ✔ clock or watch with second hand

Fashion a pendulum by tying a metal washer to a long piece of string or thread. Slide the upper end of the thread into a slit in a tongue depressor or attach it to a paper clip. Then tape the paper clip or tongue depressor to the top of a door frame, as shown in Figure 16.

Pull the washer to one side and release it from a known height above the floor. Watch it make one complete cycle, or period—over and back. To what height above the floor does it rise on the other end of its swing?

Galileo noticed that a pendulum bob (the weight at the end of the string) rises to very nearly the same height on one side of its swing as it does on the other. Of course, the swing gradually diminishes and eventually stops,

FIGURE 16

tongue depressor,
Popsicle stick,
or paper clip

door frame

tape

thread

washer

but Galileo believed that if there were no friction, the bob would continue to swing back and forth forever. From this he reasoned that if a block or ball were to slide down a frictionless incline, it would rise to the same height on a second incline, just as a pendulum bob does in its swing. If the second incline were made longer and less steep, the ball would travel farther before starting its return. If there were no second incline, but only a horizontal plane, the ball, reasoned Galileo, would continue to move indefinitely. "After all," he asked, "what force would stop it if there were no friction?"

It was Galileo who first realized that a body in motion will continue to move at the same speed unless some force changes its motion. Usually there are frictional forces that cause a body to slow down. Of course, he argued, if a body is at rest (speed = 0), it will stay at rest unless acted upon by some force.

In Galileo's time there were no clocks outside of church towers, but he realized that a pendulum could be used to keep very good time. To see why, set your pendulum in motion and measure its period—the time it takes the pendulum to make one complete swing, over and back. It is difficult to measure a single period, so use a clock or watch to time 10 or

100 swings, then divide the number of seconds by 10 or 100. For instance, if the pendulum makes 100 swings in two minutes (120 seconds), its period is 120 seconds/100, which is 1.2 seconds per swing. If it makes 100 swings in only one minute, its period is 0.6 second per swing.

Determine the period of your pendulum. Then let it swing for several minutes and determine its period again. Has it changed? Do you see why Galileo regarded the pendulum as a good way to keep time? Have you ever seen a clock with a pendulum?

Measure the length of your pendulum from the point of support at the top to the center of the washer. Add a second washer to the bob so that its weight doubles, but keep the length exactly the same. Does the weight of the pendulum bob affect its period?

Does the length of the pendulum affect its period? How can you find out?

How about the amplitude of its swing—the distance that it moves? Does that affect its period?

Experiment 4.6*

PENDULUMS THAT DANCE AND TWIST

To do this experiment you will need:

✔ string

✔ yardstick or meterstick

✔ steel washers

✔ tape

✔ chair, table, or door frame

✔ pencil or thin stick

Pendulums are all around us. Watch a hook swinging from a crane. You can determine its length quite accurately by timing its swing. Watch a hanging plant or wind chimes in a breeze. Or watch the slow swing of a giraffe's or an elephant's long legs as it walks. Compare their period with the rapid natural motion of a small dog's legs. Compare the gaits of a professional basketball center and a young child.

Hang two pendulums of equal length (about 2 feet), and with equal weight bobs, side by side from a chair, tabletop, or door frame. They should be about 15 cm (6 in) apart (see Figure 17). As you can see, they will swing with the same period.

FIGURE 17

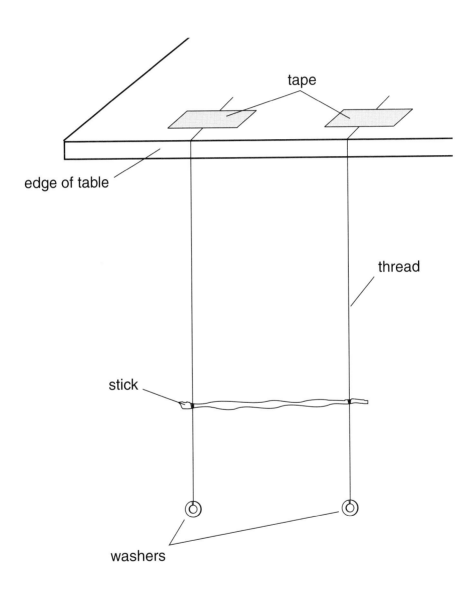

tape

edge of table

thread

stick

washers

Connect the two pendulums with a thin stick or pencil. Wind each pendulum's string around the stick once about a foot above the bobs. Pull one bob to the side and let go. Notice how it transfers its motion to the other bob because of their connection.

To make the pendulum do a twisting dance, move the stick down closer to the bobs. What happens now after you start one pendulum?

What happens if you change the weight of one bob by adding more washers?

Experiment 4.7

Things Tend to Stay Put

To do this experiment you will need:

- ✔ 3-in x 5-in index card or playing card
- ✔ cup or glass
- ✔ coin or washer
- ✔ table or counter
- ✔ water
- ✔ plastic dishes
- ✔ newspaper or smooth cloth
- ✔ silverware

The idea that objects at rest tend to remain at rest is one that Galileo probably came to by doing experiments like the following.

Place an index card or playing card on top of a cup or drinking glass. Put a coin or washer on the center of the card. With a sharp flick of your finger, drive the card off the cup. Or, if you find it easier to do, give the card a quick pull. What happens to the coin? Does it tend to remain at rest?

Place the index card on the edge of a table or counter. About one third of the card should project out beyond the edge. Put some water in a plastic cup or glass and place it on the other two thirds of the card. Give the card a quick pull toward you. What happens to the water-filled cup? Does it stay in place?

Now that you are confident that things do tend to stay in place, you may be ready to try a "trick" you have probably seen on television or in a movie. Cover part of a table or counter with a newspaper or smooth cloth. Set the table with a plate, cup and saucer, and silverware. With a sharp yank, pull the "tablecloth" out from under the utensils, leaving them undisturbed on the table. (It is a good idea to use plastic dishes until you are an expert at this experiment.)

Experiment 4.8

THINGS IN MOTION CONTINUE IN MOTION

To do this experiment you will need:

✔ an ADULT	✔ glue
✔ 1/16-in bit and drill	✔ empty thread spool
✔ 7.5-cm (3-in) square or circle of 1/4-in plywood or Masonite	✔ balloon
✔ sandpaper	✔ smooth Formica countertop

As his first law of motion Sir Isaac Newton used Galileo's idea that the motion of a body (at rest or moving) tends to be maintained. This is commonly known as the law of inertia—the idea that the motion of a body can be changed only by applying a force, a push or a pull.

You have seen that bodies at rest tend to stay at rest unless a force is applied, but it is more difficult to demonstrate that a body in motion tends to maintain its motion. Usually, frictional forces cause a body to slow down and stop unless we apply a force greater than or equal to the friction. That is why your moving bicycle will stop unless you pedal; it is why a car comes to a stop unless the engine is used to keep the wheels turning.

A pendulum's motion is nearly frictionless, but it is a back-and-forth motion. By building an "air car" you can see virtually frictionless motion along a straight line.

To build such a car, **ask an adult** to help you drill a 1/16-in hole in the very center of a 1/4-in-thick piece of plywood or Masonite. The thin piece of wood can be either a square about 6 to 7 cm (2 ½ to 3 in) on a side or a circle with a similar diameter.

Use sandpaper to make one side of the wood very smooth. The outside edges of the wood should be sanded to round them off.

Glue one end of an empty spool (there may be one in your sewing kit) to the unsanded side of the square or disk. Be sure the hole in the spool is directly over the hole in the wood. See Figure 18.

When the glue is thoroughly dry, attach an inflated balloon to the spool and place the air car on a smooth Formica countertop. Air emerging from beneath the wood will provide a thin air space between wood and counter. Give the car a push. Notice how it moves with

FIGURE 18

no sign of slowing down unless it comes to a hill.

You see evidence of inertia in your daily life. If you are riding in a car, train, or bus that stops suddenly, you tend to keep moving forward. In an automobile you feel the seat belt, which is attached to the car, holding you back when this happens. That is why seat belts are helpful in accidents: They prevent people from continuing to move, through a windshield, for example.

Ice on a highway reduces the friction between tires and road so that cars tend to continue to move straight when they come to a curve and so slide off the road.

On a seesaw, you tend to keep going up after your partner's end of the board hits the ground. When it is your turn to go down, you feel the bump as you tend to keep going after your end of the seesaw hits the ground.

Experiment 4.9

FALLING AT CONSTANT SPEED

To do this experiment you will need:

- ✔ salt
- ✔ water
- ✔ tall jar
- ✔ egg
- ✔ baster or funnel and tubing that fits funnel spout
- ✔ food coloring

You have seen that when an object falls, its speed increases; it accelerates like a car that is speeding up. Since the motion of a falling body is changing, there must be a force acting on it; otherwise it would continue to move with the same speed. But you have also seen that a piece of paper does not fall as fast as a ball. Friction with the air seems to slow its fall. In fact, any object falling through the air will eventually stop accelerating and reach a steady speed—its terminal velocity. When sky divers jump from an airplane, they fall faster and faster until they reach a speed of about 193 km/hr (120 mph). At that speed, the upward force due to friction with the air becomes equal to the force of gravity pulling them downward.

You can see a similar effect if you release an egg in a tall jar of water. The egg soon reaches its terminal velocity as it falls. Try it and see.

But what will happen if the egg falls into a fluid in which it will float? Can you guess?

To test your prediction, prepare a saturated solution of salt in water—about 12 ounces (350 grams) per quart of water. Will an egg float in this solution? You can put a layer of salt water below some tap water in a tall jar using a funnel and tubing (see Figure 19) or a basting syringe. Pour the salt water slowly so that it disturbs the water above as little as possible. You might like to add food coloring to the solution so that you can easily distinguish it from the water. What happens when you drop the egg into the layered liquids? Where else have you seen this effect?

FIGURE 19

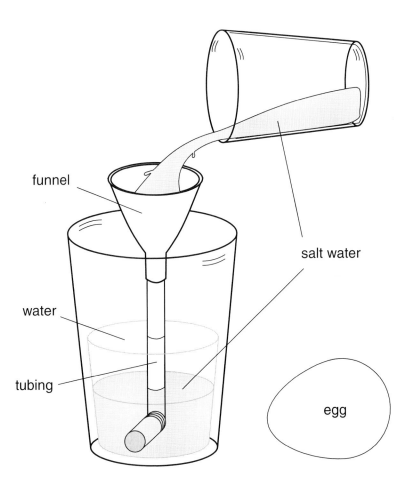

funnel

salt water

water

tubing

egg

Experiment 4.10

UP OR DOWN?

To do this experiment you will need:

✔ tall glass jar or bottle

✔ eyedropper

✔ water

✔ rubber stopper or cork that fits mouth of jar or bottle

Many things in the natural world fall and reach a terminal velocity—dust, leaves, raindrops, snowflakes, paper, and sky divers. Objects falling in water usually reach a terminal velocity very quickly, but there are some things, such as submarines, that can move up and down. Here is a submarine that you can make for yourself.

Fill a jar with water. Leave about an inch or two for air at the top. Draw enough water into an eyedropper so that it floats in the jar with just the top of its rubber bulb above water.

Place the cork or stopper in the mouth of the jar. What happens to the eyedropper when you push down on the stopper? What happens when you release, lift, or remove the stopper from the jar? Can you make the "submarine" stay in the middle of the water so that it neither sinks nor floats? How do you explain the eyedropper's behavior when you push or pull on the stopper?

Experiment 4.11*

THE WAY THE BALL BOUNCES

To do this experiment you will need:

✔ different kinds of balls; e.g., tennis, golf, baseball, rubber, Ping-Pong, marble, clay, Superball	✔ freezer
	✔ cookie sheet
	✔ oven
✔ yardstick or meterstick	✔ tongs, large forceps, or pot holders
✔ different surfaces; e.g., wood, concrete, tile, carpeting, newspaper, loose wood	✔ an ADULT

Drop a ball from a height of 90 cm (36 in) onto a hard floor. How high does it bounce? You will have to get your head down beside the yardstick to see how high the bottom of the ball rises. Why should you always make your measurements from the bottom of the ball? (*Hint:* How far does the ball actually fall and rise?)

You will find the experiment a lot easier to do if you have someone help you. One person can drop the ball while the other watches to see how high it bounces.

What fraction of its original height does the ball attain on its first bounce? On its second bounce?

If you drop the ball from the height to which it rose on its first bounce, can you predict how high it will bounce this time? Can you predict how high it will bounce if you drop it from a height of 46 cm (18 in)? Of 30 cm (12 in)?

Try dropping other kinds of balls onto the same surface. Which kind of ball is the bounciest? Which one is the least bouncy? (Did you try a ball of clay?) Which ball do you think will keep bouncing for the longest time?

Do you think the kind of surface the balls land on will have any effect on their bounce heights? To find out, try the same experiment on different surfaces such as concrete, tile, and carpeting. What do you find? Can you explain your results?

You may find it helpful, as you think about your results, to try dropping a ball on a firm wooden floor and then on a piece of wood balanced on two bricks or blocks.

To see if temperature has any effect on a ball's bounciness, first see how high the different balls bounce at room temperature. Then place the balls in a freezer (or outdoors if it is very cold) for about an hour. Remove the balls one at a time and test their bounciness. Has the lower temperature changed the bounciness of any of the balls?

Can you predict what will happen to the bounciness of the balls if they are heated?

Ask an adult to help you test your predictions by placing the balls on a cookie sheet and heating them in a warm (not hot) oven for a few minutes.

When the balls are warm, use tongs, forceps, or pot holders to remove them from the oven one at a time and test each ball for bounciness.

Are any of the balls bouncier than before? If they are, do they retain their bouncier nature after they cool?

If you have not tried it yet, roll a piece of clay into a ball and drop it. Examine the clay carefully after it has fallen. Compare its shape with that of the other balls you dropped. Can you explain why the clay behaved differently?

What can you do to make a ball bounce higher than the height from which it is released? Is it easier to do this for some balls than for others? Are there any for which this is impossible?

FALLING SIDEWAYS

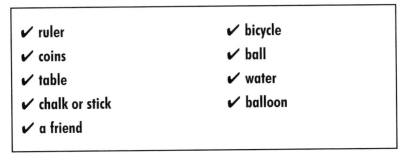

To do this experiment you will need:

✔ ruler	✔ bicycle
✔ coins	✔ ball
✔ table	✔ water
✔ chalk or stick	✔ balloon
✔ a friend	

Galileo once asked what would happen if a sailor dropped a stone into the water from the high mast of a moving ship. Would the stone land at a point directly below where it was released, or would it continue to move forward with the ship and land directly below the moving sailor?

He also wondered if the time it took the stone to fall would be different than if it had been dropped without any horizontal motion.

You can find the answers to Galileo's questions by doing the following experiments.

Place a coin on the edge of a table or counter. Place a second identical coin on the end of a ruler that projects out beyond the edge of the table. Put your index finger on the midpoint of the ruler. Use your other hand to give the ruler a sharp nudge toward the table, as shown in Figure 20. The end of the ruler on the table should drive the coin at the table's edge horizontally outward. The other end of the ruler should move out from under the coin because the coin's inertia will make it stay put. Thus, one coin will fall straight down to the floor, while the other one will move horizontally as it falls. Which coin do you think will strike the floor first? Or will both coins land at the same time?

You can find the answer by listening carefully after you release the coins. Do you hear two distinct sounds as they land or just one?

Draw a target on your sidewalk, path, or driveway with chalk or a stick. Ask a friend to ride a bike over the spot and drop a ball or a water balloon when he or she is directly above the target. Watch closely. Does the ball or balloon fall straight down and hit the target? Or does it continue to move with the bike and land beyond target?

Now you get on your bike and try it. Where should you release the ball if you want it to hit the target?

FIGURE 20

Finger holds ruler
firmly against
table top.

flat ruler

Coin will be projected
horizontally as it falls.

table

Strike ruler
here.

Coin will
fall straight
down to floor.

Drop a bouncy ball as you walk over a hard floor. Do you have to stop to catch the ball as it bounces up or can you keep on walking and still catch it?

Try it again, but this time stop *immediately after* you release the ball. What happens to the ball?

Watch the water coming from a hose that is held so that the water emerges horizontally. If you could isolate a drop and let it fall from the nozzle of the hose, would it hit the ground before, after, or at the same time as a drop that was projected horizontally in the stream?

You can answer the last question based on what you have seen in earlier experiments. Can you also answer Galileo's questions?

On the moon the force of gravity is only one-sixth as strong as it is on Earth. If you threw a ball on the moon, would it travel as far as it does on Earth or would it travel farther?

A boy is standing on the rear platform of a train that is going 97 km/hr (60 mph). At the instant he passes you, as you stand on a platform beside the tracks, he throws a ball straight back, away from the train. The boy can throw the ball at a speed of 97 km/hr (60 mph). What path will you see the ball follow? What path will the ball follow as seen by the boy?

5

Pushes and Pulls Along Floors and Counters

If you saw a book begin to slide along a table without being pushed, or a ball begin to bounce without having fallen, you might think poltergeists were at work. Certainly something unnatural would be happening. But why would you think so?

Sir Isaac Newton provided the answer more than three hundred years ago. He realized that objects move only when forces (pushes and pulls) are applied. He also noticed that when a force acts on an object, that object accelerates positively or negatively (speeds up or slows down). Sometimes accelerations are not easy to detect. You will be able to understand acceleration better if you build an accelerometer. It will indicate the direction of the acceleration as well as its presence.

Experiment 5.1

TWO KINDS OF ACCELEROMETERS

To do this experiment you will need:

✔ carpenter's level	✔ pin
✔ tall pill bottle with cap	✔ cork
✔ water	✔ tape
✔ soap	✔ half-pint jar with screw-on cap
✔ thread	

You can use a small carpenter's level as an accelerometer, or you can build something similar by filling a tall pill bottle with water. Leave a little space at the top so there will be a bubble when you put the cap on. A tiny piece of soap in the bottle will prevent the bubble in your bubble accelerometer from sticking to the sides of the bottle. See Figure 21.

To build a cork accelerometer, tie a piece of thread to the head of a straight pin. Stick the pin into a small cork or a piece of Styrofoam. Tape the free end of the thread to the center of the screw-on cap of a clear glass or plastic jar.

FIGURE 21

BUBBLE ACCELEROMETER

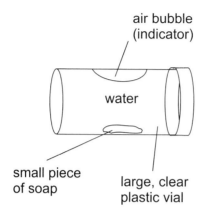

air bubble
(indicator)

water

small piece
of soap

large, clear
plastic vial

CORK ACCELEROMETER

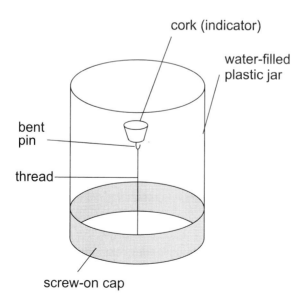

cork (indicator)

water-filled
plastic jar

bent
pin

thread

screw-on cap

Fill the jar brimful of water, screw on the cap, and invert the jar. Presto! You have an accelerometer.

Place an accelerometer on a countertop and move it gently back and forth. Watch what happens when you start or stop moving the accelerometer. Notice that the cork or bubble moves in the direction of the acceleration. The acceleration is always in the direction of the force—with the motion to start, against the motion to stop. Remember, to stop a body the force has to oppose the motion. The acceleration must be negative; that is, there must be a decrease in speed.

Take an accelerometer on a walk. Be sure to keep it level. Do you accelerate as you walk?

With an adult, take an accelerometer for an automobile ride. Can it detect accelerations in the car? Do any of the directions surprise you?

Experiment 5.2

BIG AND LITTLE PULLS

To do this experiment you will need:

✔ accelerometer	✔ identical rubber bands or sensitive spring scale
✔ fairly heavy toy truck or small wagon	✔ ruler

Mount an accelerometer on a toy truck or a small wagon. Attach a rubber band or a spring scale to the front of the truck or wagon. How big a stretch is needed to make the vehicle move along with a slow but constant speed? This is the minimum force needed to overcome friction. (You can measure the stretch on a rubber band by placing it above a ruler as you pull it.)

Pull the toy again. This time stretch the rubber band more than enough to overcome friction. Keep the rubber band stretched the same amount as you pull. What happens to the truck's or wagon's speed as you pull? What does your accelerometer indicate?

Repeat these steps, but double the force by stretching *two* side-by-side rubber bands as much as you stretched one before. What happens to the acceleration as the force gets bigger?

Experiment 5.3

FORCE, MATTER, AND MORE MATTER

To do this experiment you will need:

✔ materials from
Experiment 5.2

✔ some weights to add to
the truck or wagon

What do you think will happen to the acceleration of your truck or wagon if you add more weight to it without changing the force?

Test your prediction by first accelerating the vehicle with a certain force. Then add weight so that the amount of matter is at least doubled. Repeat the experiment using the same force. What happens to the acceleration of the truck? Were you right?

MAKING THINGS GO ROUND AND ROUND

To do this experiment you will need:

- ✔ accelerometer
- ✔ record player turntable or lazy Susan
- ✔ cardboard
- ✔ scissors
- ✔ clear tape
- ✔ marking pen

You probably were not surprised to find that heavy things move more sluggishly than lighter ones given the same force. Nor were you startled to learn that bigger forces give bigger accelerations. After all, you know that you can accelerate a tennis ball a lot more easily than a bowling ball, and that a tennis ball will attain greater speed if you hit it harder.

The interesting thing is that Newton used this simple understanding of force and acceleration to explain the movement of the planets and stars as well as that of falling bodies and horse-drawn carriages. In fact, he used it to explain all motion.

But planets move about the sun in near circles with nearly constant speed. Can a force be acting on them if they are moving at constant speed?

You can do a simple experiment to find out. Hold an accelerometer at arm's length (be sure it is level) and turn around, watching the accelerometer as you turn. What do you find?

To see what is happening in more detail, tape an accelerometer to a turntable or lazy Susan. When the table turns at a steady speed, is there an acceleration?

Were you surprised? What was the direction of the acceleration? What must have been the direction of the force?

To see if the acceleration is related to the speed, change the speed of the turntable, or move the accelerometer closer to and then farther from the center of the spinning table. Where is the speed of a spinning table greatest? Where is its speed zero?

How is the acceleration affected by the speed?

See if you can predict the direction of the acceleration on a playground merry-go-round, a toy train moving along a circular track, or a car rounding a curve.

By the way, have you ever tried to draw a straight line on a spinning turntable?

Cut a piece of cardboard to fit the turntable and fasten it on with tape.

Can you figure out a way to draw a circle on a spinning table? It is really very easy. But try to draw a straight line from the center to the edge of the table while it is turning.

Not so easy, is it? Can you figure out a way to do it? (*Hint:* How does the speed of any point on the table change as you move outward from the center?)

Experiment 5.5*

An Inward Force

To do this experiment you will need:

✔ plastic pail	✔ water

Newton knew that an inward acceleration indicated an inward force. He also realized that a force was needed to change the *direction* of a circling body's motion. After all, a change in direction is as significant as a change in speed.

The inward force causing something to move in a circle is called a centripetal force. You can feel such a force by doing the following experiment.

Fill a plastic pail about one-fourth full of water. Take it outdoors or someplace where you can swing it without hitting anything or having to worry about spilling.

Swing the pail in a *vertical* circle that extends from over your head to very near the ground, as shown in Figure 22. (Do not worry, the water will stay in the pail.) You will feel the force your arm exerts to keep the pail moving in a circle.

From what you already know about acceleration in circular motion, would you expect the required force to increase or decrease if you swung the pail faster? Try it. Were you right?

If you add more water to the pail, will the force needed for circular motion at the same speed be greater, less, or the same? Try it.

FIGURE 22

pail with water

Why do you think water stays in the pail even while it is upside down? (*Hint:* Suppose the centripetal acceleration of the pail is greater than the acceleration due to gravity.)

Perhaps you have gone through a loop-the-loop on a roller coaster. If you have, then you know what it is like to be the water in the pail.

THE PUSH/PUSH BACK LAW

To do this experiment you will need:

✔ 2 toy trucks or cars	✔ weights
✔ tape	✔ rubber band
✔ spring-type clothespin	

When you swing a pail in a circle, you have to pull it inward to constantly change its direction. But you can feel the pail pulling outward on your arm. If you and a friend are on roller skates or ice skates and you give your friend a push, he or she will move away from you. At the same time, you too will move, but in the opposite direction.

Again, it was Newton who first realized that forces always come in pairs. If you push on something living or nonliving, that thing pushes back on you with an equal force in the opposite direction. This is Newton's third law of motion, but we will call it the push/push back law.

To see this law in action, without being directly involved in the pushing, try this experiment. Find two toy cars or trucks that are reasonably large. Tape a spring-type clothespin upside down to the front of one of the trucks or cars. Push the vehicles together to compress the spring, as shown in Figure 23. Release both cars at the same time. Does Newton's law seem to apply?

What do you think will happen if you repeat the experiment after adding some weight to one of the trucks? Try it. Which truck moved faster? Does it make any difference which truck is heavier?

Replace one truck with something much heavier, such as a wall. Stretch the clothespin spring by pushing the truck against the wall. Now the pushes are between the truck and the earth. (After all, the wall is part of the house, which is firmly attached to the earth.) What do you find when you release the truck? What do you think will happen to the truck's speed after release if you add weight to the truck?

Try to predict what will happen if you give the truck, with the clothespin attached and open, a push so that it collided with the other identical truck. How will the push given by the moving truck affect the stationary truck? How will the truck at rest change the motion of the

FIGURE 23

moving truck? Remember, Newton said the pushes will be equal but opposite in direction.

What happens if one truck is heavier than the other? Does it matter whether the moving or stationary truck is heavier? What happens if the truck collides with the wall (earth)?

From what you have learned about collisions, how do you think cars and highways might be designed in order to make them safer?

When you walk or run, you get your push *forward* by pushing your feet *backward* against the earth. Does your push on the earth make the earth move? What happens when you try to step from an untied rowboat onto a dock? When you try to walk on very slippery ice? When you walk in loose sand?

Do you think Newton's law applies to pulls as well as pushes? To find out, connect your two trucks with a stretched rubber band so that they pull on each other when you release them. Using pulls instead of pushes, repeat the other experiments above. Are the results similar?

Experiment 5.7

A ROCKET BOAT

To do this experiment you will need:

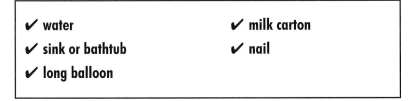

- ✔ water
- ✔ sink or bathtub
- ✔ long balloon
- ✔ milk carton
- ✔ nail

A rocket is an example of the push/push back law. You can make a "rocket boat" as shown in Figure 24. Make the hole in the back of the boat, through which you pull the mouth of the balloon, small enough so that the "fuel" will last for several seconds. What happens when you release the rocket? How does the rocket demonstrate Newton's law?

Experiment 5.8*

Friction: Something That Is Always With Us

To do this experiment you will need:

- ✔ washers
- ✔ thread
- ✔ smooth board
- ✔ wooden blocks
- ✔ paper clips
- ✔ sandpaper
- ✔ aluminum foil
- ✔ waxed paper
- ✔ thumb tacks
- ✔ rubber bands
- ✔ newspaper
- ✔ tape
- ✔ construction paper
- ✔ round pencils
- ✔ ruler

In most of your experiments so far, you have kept frictional forces small by using cars on wheels, marbles, and motions in air. But in most normal activities friction plays an important, often vital, part. Imagine what it would be like to try to walk without friction between your feet and the floor or ground, or of how useless cars, buses, and trains would be without friction.

Galileo and Newton were able to understand motion better than others because they could understand what motion would be like *without* friction. But they both knew that friction was a force that always acted against motion. You saw what frictionless motion is like when you used your air car (Chapter 4).

Friction is always present when one surface moves over another. But you have probably noticed that frictional forces vary with different kinds of surfaces. For example, it is much easier to walk over a rubber mat than over a polished floor or an icy sidewalk.

You can use the simple friction tester shown in Figure 25 to measure the friction between surfaces. Place a block on a smooth board and add washers to the hook until the block slides with a steady speed. The number of washers required to move the block is a measure of the friction opposing the motion.

Does it take more washers to make the block begin to move than it does to keep it moving once started?

If you find starting friction greater than the friction present once the block is in motion, try tapping the board as you add washers to free the block.

Is friction related to weight? To find out, put a second, identical block on the first one,

FIGURE 25

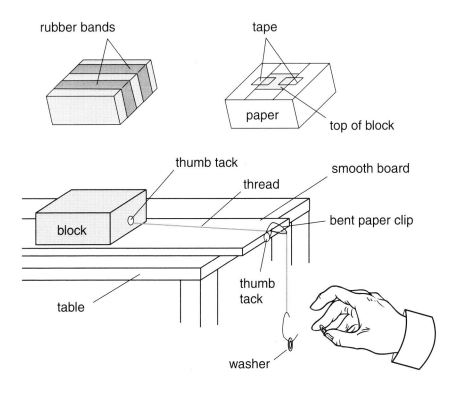

or add weights equal to the weight of the block. Is the friction greater? Is it twice as great?

Does the area of the surfaces rubbing together affect friction? If the block is smooth on all sides, turn it so that it rests on a narrower side and see if it changes the number of washers you must add to make the block slide. If the block is not as smooth on its narrow side, cover it with a smooth material—

aluminum foil or newspaper, for instance—
then test the effect of changing the area. What
do you find?

Tape a sheet of newspaper to the block. How
many washers are needed to make the block
slide now?

Repeat the experiment but cover the bottom
of the block with aluminum foil, waxed paper,
or construction paper. You can put wide rubber
bands around the block to make a rubber
surface. You can also change the surface of the
board by taping various things such as
aluminum foil to it. You can test to see the
effect of putting the block on rollers (round
pencils work well). Try a variety of surfaces
and keep a record of your results. What pair of
surfaces provide the most friction? The least?

Another way to test friction is to raise the
board as you tap it. Raise one end of the board
until the block slides. Then measure the height
you lifted the board or the angle it makes with
the tabletop. Do your results on this test agree
with those of your earlier experiment?

FURTHER READING

Bonnet, Robert L., and Dan Keen. *Science Fair Projects: Physics*. New York: Sterling Publishing Company, 1999.

Cobb, Vicki, and Kathy Darling. *You Gotta Try This!: Absolutely Irresistible Science*. New York: Morrow Junior Books, 1999.

Friedhoffer, Robert. *Physics Lab in the Home*. New York: Franklin Watts, 1997

Moje, Steven W. *Cool Chemistry: Great Experiments with Simple Stuff*. New York: Sterling Publishing Company, 1999.

INTERNET ADDRESSES

Ask a Scientist Archive
<http://newton.dep.anl.gov/archive.htm>

Chem4Kids
<http://www.chem4kids.com>

Internet Public Library: Your Science Fair Project
   Resource Guide
<http://www.ipl.org/youth/projectguide>

Playground Physics
<http://lyra.colorado.edu/sbo/mary/play>

The Ultimate Science Fair Resource
<http://www.scifair.org>

INDEX